WRITERS REPUBLIC

WELCOME HOME
LITTLE
POLTERGEIST

words, photographs, sketches

VINCENT HOLLOW

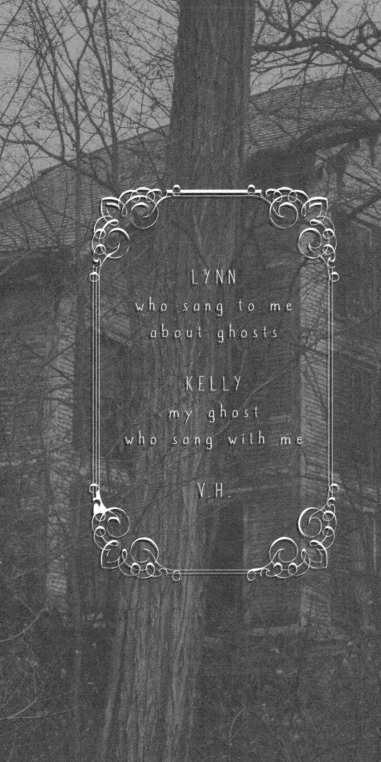

LYNN
who sang to me
about ghosts

KELLY
my ghost
who sang with me

V.H.

WRITERS REPUBLIC L.L.C.
515 Summit Ave. Unit R1
Union City, NJ 07087, USA

Website: *www.writersrepublic.com*
Hotline: *1-877-656-6838*
Email: *info@writersrepublic.com*

Ordering Information:
Quantity sales. Special discounts are available on quantity purchases by corporations, associations, and others. For details, contact the publisher at the address above.

Library of Congress Control Number: 2020952528
ISBN-13:   978-1-63728-124-6   [Paperback Edition]
                  978-1-63728-125-3   [Hardback Edition]
                  978-1-63728-126-0   [Digital Edition]

Rev. date: 12/16/2020

WELCOME HOME LITTLE POLTERGEIST

WELCOME

it's so hard
watching you disappear
like a reel of film
being gradually exposed
until each frame is only white fog
erasing all of your exquisite details

your sparkling eyes
with their deep shadow outlines
strands of your cimmerian hair
pink lips glistening like rosé in a crystal chalice
until only a pale silhouette
stands against a horizon of clouds and memory

blinding white lights of your aura
my eyes straining
hoping for one last glimpse
of your hazel moons
that have given me the sweetest of dreams
on the darkest nights
for all eternity

Films About Ghosts

sparrows sing like a children's choir
between golden cello and viola grasses
riding the morning mist
to rest on pews of broken branches

you woke without me
and walked out into the fields
summer symphonies dissipated
an everlasting equinox revealed

The End of Summer

every year
the trees ignite
and I retrieve their flames
for your funeral pyre
and dance while the ashes rain
and my skin melts away

how do you love
a ghost?
how can you hold on
to the one you lost?
it's too quiet here
only the sound of the breeze
and your breathing
fills my ears
it's nearly dawn again
and I haven't slept

Love A Ghost

it's that time of year again
when I must leave wherever I call home
and go in search of another
a little bit further away
in a quieter part of Nowhere
but somehow
always within reach of you

Quieter Part of Nowhere

you are my favorite urban legend
a ghost story told at bonfires
and prom night parking lots
on certain nights
I can find the truth in these tales
your song wandering a moonlit street
searching for a place you used to live
I try to catch you
so I can hold you again
but your presence slowly wanes
still
it doesn't stop me from trying

Urban Legend

young enough
to remember yesterday
old enough to miss it
knowing I can never return
but maybe someday
I can visit
and maybe
I will see her

Visit Yesterday

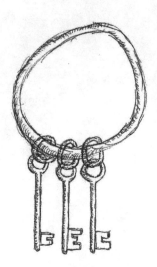

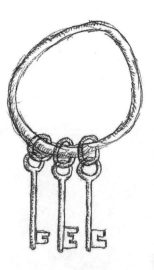

how will it be
five years from now
when the taste of you
abandons from my tongue?

how will it feel
without your voice in my mouth?
I didn't mean to misplace you
to the place where the vampires have hung

In Five Years

birds begin their migrations
it's not worth it to stay here
when all of your friends
are leaving their sinking foundations

everything is turning to dust
and the air grows cold
with every day
decaying like rust

as the seasons pass, I silently grieve
I see the flocks from my bedroom
and think perhaps
I should leave too

Migrate

behind this envelope
I've built myself a camp
just me and a lamp
sealed with hope

I left myself a trail of crumbs
what have I become
to find my way back home
lost on this hidden road?

but the crows
in their caliginous clothes
took my trail of bread
and silently fed

The Crows

to wake up alive
lips loosely sewn
the ceiling low
the night slow
I'm afraid
of the new day
oh, how the sun shone
when you woke up alive

Wake Up Alive

a heart to mend
your eyelash flutter
memento with no end
yearning for my departed lover

no hands of time
only fingers
a creeping vine
a gravedigger

its damage concealed
in the movements of a mime
minutes slowly congealed
in the spaces of my spine

Gravedigger

a visionary psychopath
my momentary relapse
the silence when beds collapse
and we become necromantic acrobats

palms cut with glass
knees stained with grass
finding my way back
to our home of poltergeists and Prozac

Poltergeists and Prozac

I watch films of your ghost
reeling at your haunting beauty
and recording my nightmares
for the world to see
our dreams of the diseased
it's no wonder
why I'm always awake

Films About Ghosts
Reel 2

oh, the howling
it is the song of the sobbing moon
and dying stars falling
I cry with the lycan
hoping to catch a star
like a snowflake
as it falls

you feel
what no one else can
a stubborn numbness
the nerves in your fingers
severed with shears
dangling like tinsel

they tell you to hold on
but how will you know when
you have it in your hands
if everything
slips through?

Numb

no matter how much
I may tell you to leave
I covet your invisible touch
where our phalanges weave

Invisible

don't stop
don't ever stop digging
your nails are spades
they forgot to hammer them in

don't stop
don't ever stop digging
from the earth, you shall evade
and be home in the morning

Don't Stop Digging

24

in this hourglass of moonlight
how I love watching those cosmic crystals
shimmer like sugar stars

they taste like you did

as I kiss them from the sky
my mouth spills sunlight waterfalls
and antique mirror shards

Sugar Star Kiss

I want to bathe in ectoplasm
the residues of the resurrected
absorb the tears of the tombs
until my body becomes a catacomb

crawling with zombified memories
squirming and moaning
as they consume my lovely brain
and leave my skull a vacant shell

Vacancy

these chains
will never tear us apart
they'll only leave us
in pieces

how can I cross oceans for you
when I'm so afraid of drowning?
how can I leave them all behind
if their wails keep resounding?

how can I speak in tongues
when mine was caught in the gates?
how can I find my way home
if it's constantly changing place?

Drowning

make a model of the home
we've never lived
built in our dreams
where our ruins take up residence

a cassette clicks
the chime of bicycle bells
and nursery rhymes
play to jump rope rhythms

the house waits
watching with doll's eyes
until we wake
and walk inside

Model Home

eventually
everyone fades
but you
and your shade

but even shadows
disappear at night
returning at dawn
with the coming of the light

Eventually...

it's nearly six o'clock
at the lookout in our Cadillac
you awaken in the backseat
deep wells of starlight remnants
collide with my moon crater stare
I join you in the back
to have this morning in your arms
the sunrise came and went
and you closed your eyes once more

This Mourning Together

driving on quiet thoughts
voice tied up in knots
reaching that lane
just past the trains
shaded by trees
and memories

our house rests
blue and depressed
body left out in the rain
smoke in the windowpane
missing curtains
something burning

paranormal sighting
always inviting
the door still open
stuck in that moment
but I know
there's nobody home

Nobody Home

I'll always miss you
I gently kiss you
sealing our love notes
where your body floats

I'll never leave you
in my slumber, I feel you
the river flows by my home
I hear you sleepwalk through the snow

the love of a thousand centuries
dwelling in those memories
where you and I float
me and my ghost

Me and My Ghost

when signs read

DO NOT ENTER.

all I see is

COME IN.
WE'VE BEEN WAITING.

love and death
are homes with
the warmest welcomes

home
is where the heart is
and where
your ghosts live

you were married to the void
and I was your boy
of the abyss
dark and deep
awaiting your kiss of crows

I can't stop resurrecting you
filling vial upon vial
with elixirs of your evanescence
conjuring your essence in nocturnal spells
of lavender blooming under moonbeams
the aroma of sage burning from raging stars
September's solitude leads to October's obituary
will you live long enough this time
for me to hear your voice again
outside of my dreams?

Evanescent Elixirs

with the wolves crying
their soporific songs
to soothe my somnolent heart
serenade this love undying
of a heart I know isn't gone
of souls that should never part

Howling Heart

the memory of skin
coated with graveyard dirt
and werewolf fur
the dead buried within
leaving mud on my shirt
and blood on your skirt

Memory of Skin

I enter on a dare
should I be this scared
despite the spiders in my spine?
this house was never all mine

groaning of rotten doors
the chord of a Krzysztof score
greeting ghosts in oil paintings
how long have you been waiting?

the fragrance of decay
all the words we'd say
hanging nooses on the air
should I be this scared?

Reasonable Fear

we all come back
eventually
gradually

we'll come back
someday
someway

welcome back
did you miss me?
do you remember how
you'd kiss me?

Welcome Home

some people
go missing
on purpose

every night
I'm watching you
on an old VHS tape
in the middle of a movie
I don't remember starting

in a scene with missing dialogue
there will be a moment
of this played-out screenplay
when you turn a corner
and I rush to follow

but the scene cuts
the location shifts
to somewhere we've been before
but slightly askew
and the only thing missing
is you

Cinema

failed
no, these nails
come down like hail
and seal this home now stale

I'm sore
and these doors
open no more
your footsteps on the floor

our home
stands alone
with weary bones
I sit by the telephone

it rings
rings
rings
and I give in

Ring

witness to the unknown
heavy breathing on the phone
there are no explanations
beneath the house's foundation

nothing makes sense
pumpkins impaled on the fence
grasping dog hairs and straws
wiping our eyes, collecting our jaws

Witness

I know where you are
laying in the sigh of stars
in the back of an abandoned car
humming the song of the sea
waiting for me
to meet in our reverie

Reverie

it is not trespassing
if you once called
decaying memory
a home

gasping for breath
starving for it
save me some air
suspended underwater
we could swim
but why bother?
we're both so tired
experienced in the art of sinking

The Art of Sinking

I wasn't afraid
for you to die
I was afraid
you would disappear

someone renamed the seasons
changed their sequence
how can I know how long it's been
or how far I've come in a year?
how will I know when the doors open
if you'll reappear?

cold and alone in the summer
where are the arms to cover me?
what happened to the warmth I used to hold?
I've been crawling through glass
through our house we never sold
that tormented transparent have trashed

held hostage by my own hauntings
in the grip of your ghost's cryptic calling
deep in the mausoleum of my mind
when the windows and mirrors break
spider eyes twinkle in the candlelight
this house, a home I hope to make

Hostage

the heart
is incredibly difficult
to burn
but I came prepared
with matches
and cigarettes

within
I am
without

I am made of newspaper clippings
headline streamers
of missing and neglected children
unsolved murders
with dirty, broken porcelain girls
orphaned at the scene

smudge my eyes
blur the details
fog fades to a Tuscan sun
and flakes off as ink-stained leaves
I don't want to know too much
I'm afraid to know enough

Orphaned Dolls

the house moans
like a chorus of monks
hallways play like pipe organs
in my lonely cathedral

the songs of the dead
croon all night
hoping your ghost
joins in the choir

Lonely Cathedral

like a breath
wind, soft
and sensual
kisses my neck
I listen for your whisper
telling me
you're here

Presence

I don't bother
locking our doors
how would you come in?
this house is still half yours

open doors
lead to
open arms

does your tomb
have room
for two?

I know that
you know
I'm not the reason you left
you go, yet
I follow

you don't believe
in everything you said
below, we all move slow
but time won't
it leaves with the flowerbed

hands cold
we both fled
your moans
muffled under stones
the seasons in your head

you are the reason
you forgot
how quickly we grow
and how bright we glow
how slowly the leaves rot

you make the mausoleum so majestic
extravagant in your eternal entrails
draped in autumn garland
as you tend your frail garden
hanging by your fingernails

paint the walls
a violent vermillion
from the eyes to the bones
make this house your own
are the shadows still listening?

chandeliers dangle
hearts of the stolen
illuminating crystal souls
down the darkest hole
songs from throats swollen

I wish I could live here with you
in this house of the dead
but I am still breathing
and your skin is freezing
is there still time left to mend?

House of the Dead

peering eyes
shifting in Renaissance portraits
of monarchs and conquistadors
my every move
the weight of their stare
keeping me still

there is a presence in solitude
even silence has a sound
I hear shallow breathing
I hold mine like a secret
wondering
if the other will do the same

Eyes of Conquistadors

it's good to be
home again
rooms are vacant
but I'm not
alone again

in this mannequin morgue
I'm pursued by headless figures
and five-legged arachnids
like a frightened sewer rat

I only hope the light of my torch
keeps them at bay
I want to wake up under covers
before they catch me in plastic fingers

Mannequin Morgue

moldy counters
moss lines the sink
pantry never emptied
neither was the fridge

there is no odor
of decaying delicacies
now the water is boiling
a dinner for two

you made the noodles by hand
they stick together in the pot
but you never cared for perfection
maybe that's what made you
perfect

suddenly
a door slams
I look down to a rusted pot of dirt
stirred with a termite spoon
I can still smell the tomatoes

Homemade

can ghosts haunt each other?
staying up all night
in empty rooms
in empty houses
floating eerily
above their empty bodies

terrified of something
more frightening than themselves
waiting patiently behind closet doors
to jump out and make us scream
I don't know which one of us
is the one being scared

The One Being Scared

on Memory Lane
we live isolated lives
hanging rusted frames
from preserved butterflies
filled with faded faces
and still lifes of ashtrays
shapes on staircases
shifting when I turn away

Preserved Butteflies

are you in here
my friend?
in the loneliest place?
I hear your cries
lost in the trees
sailing on gusts of autumn torture

tell me where you are
and I'll find you
a trail of dirty handprints
splattered on the stairwell
there's so many
are they all from you?

are you in here?
please answer me
you're getting fainter
is that your voice
coming from downstairs?
speak up
I can't hear you

Tell Me Where You Are

do you mourn the moon every morning
and long for the phases of the phantasms
to shine their spectres
into your noctilucine satin?

a cloud of vapor manifests
into a revenant of telepathic secrets
haunting a house of chewed fingernails
that shimmer like sequins

down the basement steps
dreary and vacant
it reminds me of you
even the fragrance

I cannot speak
there's silence in the bookcase
someone sighs in the corner
why are they wearing your face?

I Don't Like the Basement

you took my breath
and stored it in your wine cellar
now I only speak
shadows and smoke
keep them safe
forever in the dark
don't lose them to the wind and leaves
to be inhaled by someone else's lungs

Breathless

firewood and bones
gray like January
but still warm
like Valentine morning

notebooks standing
side by side
paper tombstones
in a love letter cemetery
engraved in an endless equinox
of our love's decay

Paper Tombstones

mirror, mirror
hanging tall
window to nowhere
on the wall

twisted spine
sinister smile
pale moon eyes
laying in a pile

mirror mirror
is this me?
why won't you break?
why can't I see?

Lasser Glass

I see the outlines of your face
in delicate spiderwebs
catching moonlight and starlight
dripping like dew

voices in the television
escape in a skeleton mist
white noise whispers
precede your electric kiss

White Noise

in the street light malaise
the old furniture takes the form
of your comfortable contours
tricking my mind like inanimate illusionists

is that a row of throw pillows
catching the gold from the glass
or is it you sleeping
on the living room couch?

a pile of clothes tossed on the office chair
keeps pretending to be you
with your knees held up to your chin
head tilted, half smile

and in the morning
I hope when the night returns
it is the night
you'll truly arrive

Pillows

in the fields
before the frost
buried to heal
a heart beneath a cross

from the window
I visit our secret
in the harvest row
I vow to keep it

Secret Window

I'm not all there
pieces are missing
or stolen
locked away in mausoleums
like toy chests buried under beds

with all the monsters and ghosts
I hid from in childhood blankets
expecting their fingers and claws
to drag me back

Monsters Under The Bed

I'm sorry
if I talk too much
or if I seem like I'm in a rush
to hear your voice again
but you were such a good friend

and after being away for so long
a part of me fears you'll be gone
forever this time
and these lyrics are more difficult to rhyme

I can't help how I miss you
your love, a perennial residue
sticking to my skin
always imagining where you've been

Residue

we're all searching
always
all ways

the depths of dreams and doubt
forests of photographs and fears
labyrinths of love letters lost

we're all searching
always
for some unknown soul

we're all searching
all ways
while hoping to be found

Soul Searchers

I never chose this cut
you were the closest one
raped by your rose's bud
your perfume, a potent one
the aroma of poisoned blood

Poisoned Blood

look my way
don't see me
oculus slays
wraith hearts debris

all the skeletons
made your closet
a catacomb

the secret amulet
buried beneath
layers of sentimental sediments
at the bottom of a dresser drawer

gems and metals
worn on aching wrists
that you used to tie together
behind your back

I excavate like an archaeologist
and remove the jewel, fully preserved
its sheen like headlights
to my stag eyes

I swore I saw you
appear in the glimmer
of its elemental enchantment
and my wide eyes liquefy

Amulet

on a canvas of insomnia
owllight illumes
and I breathe euphoria
in the fireplace fumes

I weep
while I laugh
I must be losing myself
within the mazes of this manor
but the lost
are always the first
to find the lost
and you've been gone
far too long

Mazes

this hallway stretches on and on
our bedroom, diminishing
to the vanishing point

this illusion
our door becoming a mote of dust
with you still on the other side

are you even aware?
this vortex manipulating us
into a separate existence

if I scream for you
will you hear me?
will you know I'm real?

I'm not even sure myself
and I'm so tired
but I keep running

Down the Hall

you cannot live
with the dead
but
you're allowed
to bring your own bed

this is the room
where it happened
one light
flickering
a shadow
and a scream

no one came
and no one left
but someone
turned out the light
leaned over me
and kissed me goodnight

Goodnight Kiss

where have we gone?
should I sleep under the stairs?
did our bed feel so wrong?
I think the mattress had too many tears

I still clean the sheets
pillows stay cold on both sides
flashbacks and records on repeat
while distant songs harmonize

Torn Mattress

all the parasites multiply
drunk on a pool of pesticide
waiting for their wings to dry

scurrying to my bedside
staring with their arthropod eyes
and suddenly, I'm paralyzed

Bed Bugs

you're a love
draped in floral bed sheets
appearing in the corner of my room
hugged by the shadows
speaking in phantom poetry
giving me haunted dreams

Sheets

our room
just how we left it
lonely sky walls
teenage graffiti on your vanity
drawn in lipstick lines

it's a long way back home
maybe I can stay
just for tonight
watch the moon watching me
while my eyes grow heavy

and I'll let the dreams pour in
just like they used to
in a golden stream of honey
how I've missed their taste
just like I've missed yours

Honey Dreams

I love watching the sky
shatter into tears of glass
slaughtering the sunlight
like a cloud of bats

the streets are cleansed
washed with the debris
out of the cracks comes the cataract
turning my room into the sea

Cataract

scabs on my knees
are these walls getting closer?
is this room getting smaller?
all these sights are sober
I can't distinguish between colors
this house is just how it left me

Scabbed Knees

LITTLE
POLTERGEIST

the blood
coursing through me
trickling
from my open
wounded heart
into yours
buried
in the floorboards
bringing you back
from a place
I could not follow
to share my skin

The Blood Brought You Back

I don't want to be without you
but I'm afraid to be around you
if only I could split myself in two
let the half that's fused with your chest
live forever bonded to your flesh
while I wander sunsets in search of stars
and the ending to our postmortem memoirs

Postmortem Memoirs

I'll be the one you haunt
if that's what you want
wherever you are
I await your postcard

across fields and forests
hours never forgot us
you're invisible
so irresistible

visit me in candlelight
ghostly eyes entangle mine
may your spirit remain
and my loneliness be slain

Killing Loneliness

I'll offer you my wounds
and my dreams
all I ask in return
is your voice
to silence my screams

Offering

you remind me of a stranger
I passed once on an empty street
early one October morning
we caught each other's eyes
in a momentary glance
a temporary trance

and as we went our separate ways
I wondered if we'd ever meet again
on some other day
in some other way
like I had with you
when you and I were strangers

Strangers

always my phantom fantasy
my princess of the paranormal
I'll do whatever you please

possess me
infest me
obsess me

find our stones side by side
our names engraved
me and you, my cyanide bride

beneath the pillars of Rome
in our pinewood rooms
we'll make ourselves a home

Princess of the Paranormal

from dawn to dusk
in ghosts we trust
exorcisms and church bells
permanent guests of abandoned hotels

from dusk to dawn
shadows on the lawn
I see you approach from my window
my skin crawls as the wind blows

In Ghosts We Trust

as I lay in tenebrism
suffocating on emptiness
I feel your fingernails
graze my neck
like a dull pendulum
and suddenly
I find the will
to breathe

Tenebrism

I don't want you to be
just another tragedy
I don't want you to flee
my amaranthine anomaly

Amaranth

I follow time on three watches
hours altered by worms
while they sleep underground

                              the maggots nearly forgot this
                                  but the hours still turn
                              while our wrists are bound

                              Forgetful Maggots

let me live
in a box under your bed
with the parasites and the cenobites
writhing and laughing among ourselves

pull the wires taught
chattering teeth
seal the eyes
open my throat in thick carmine curtains

it's so wonderful down here
in the bowels of your nightmares
where the chains dangle and chime
to your funeral song

Living with the Cenobites

I heard you scream like a devil
in my dreams of graveyard gloom
the morning was coming soon
and I feared I would wake
before you were saved

I heard you scream a midnight chill
in my dreams wher our spirits freeZe
but your voice was stolen by the breeze
and I feared I would wake
before you were saved

I chased your scream in a forest of despair
in these dreams, I'm always getting lost
I heard your echo somewhere in the fog
and I feared I would wake
before you were saved

the light of a new dawn glared
now just a whisper in my mind
your vanishing soul, I will find
and I hope when I wake
we'll both be saved

Before I Wake

the rain falls
gently kissing
the ashes
and the half of you
I couldn't burn

burnt
bricks and bones
burnt faces in our loft
ashes over my eyes
and lips
let me taste your cinders
and remind me how it burns
to love you

Burnt

the stones make my skin
grow thinner
too terrified
I let it linger

but you're not anything
you're who I write songs for
the only one
I've always longed for

you bestow to my soul
the one thing I need
everything I'm breathing
everything I bleed

an altered existence
somehow, a ghost
I want you to stay
here in our haunted home

Our Haunted Home

my ghost
my beautifully grotesque
more dreadful than all the rest
laying silent in our pine box bed
delusions of death
in your porcelain head

Beautifully Grotesque

this suit of skin
stitched like a rag doll
over pumpkin bones
I can sever any of my limbs
with a tug on my heartstrings
but I only wish
to remove my hands
so you can hold them
under the harvest moon

Pumpkin Bones

I could give you anything
but I can't give you everything
I would do anything
to be your anything

it's a curse
having all this ink
in my veins
so I must bleed
relentlessly
to complete this verse

Bleed Black

missing the dead
longing for living
kissing in bed
falling forgiving

seductress of the supernatural
won't you wake me
from these hallucinations unstable?
don't let your ghostly touch
drift like a veil of smoke
I'll miss it too damn much
I don't want to breathe anymore
unless it's your name
I don't want to open any more doors
unless it's you beyond its frame

Supernatural

the rising of the black sun
what is it that makes the horses run?
it is better to lay on the shore
where the horrors loom no more
motionless, kissed by the foam
than to stay back home

the television cracks alive
carousel plays carnival lullabies
those horses don't run away
they keep me awake
laying under an ardent tree
I never sleep

The Horses Keep Me Up

vampire in my rib cave
hanging from the bone
drink from the cantharus
of my catacomb

pitch marble eyes
reveal no pulse or soul
the mandible chews out
a wounded keyhole

pick the lock with your tongue
and savor my sanctum
tastes of sweet death
and warm aged rum

Vampire Rum

wilt into dust
coalesce in my lungs
let me breathe you in
memories on my tongue

I want to suffocate
blue as the sky and the sea
if it meant I could keep you
safe inside of me

Blue

I always want you
inside of me
in my head
behind my eyes

I breathe you in
with the spiders
and exhale cobweb lace
chanting haunting hymns

but it's not my voice
it's not my words
but I like the way they feel on my lips
and I keep them all the same

Cobweb Lace

don't turn around
it's better this way
you're not meant to see
what comes for you
what came for me

no matter
what sadistic sounds
you may hear
stay facing the corner
but don't cover your ears

Not For Your Eyes

will you meet me
on the other side?
transcend the eventide
and as you and I
arrive in the abyss
will we collide?

Eventide

all I ever wanted was you
but what else can I do?
the pain of a dozen nails
driven into my ankles

a rocking horse with hollow eyes
and a long nefarious smile
feed the centipede the dinner scraps
its head resting on my lap

what do I deserve?
I cannot feel my nerves
what else can I do?
all I ever wanted was you

All I Ever Wanted

how do my fingernails
cut so deep?
in the wounds
plant the seeds

from the veins
grows the bouquet
from the stain
our love remains

Wounded Bouquet

this body
mine and yours
terror fills my pores
why do I shake so violently?
is it the brisk November air
or the power of necromancy?

I offer you this tribute
let me bleed into your throat
and draw my wounds on your lips
in flourishing scripture
will they still taste as sweet
when the scars heal?

take this blessing
it's all I have to give
I will let my body shrivel up
as a corpse in the August afternoon
so a garden may grow
in your desert soul

Tribute

listening through the floor
to footsteps beyond the door
I cried timidly to the boards

"no more...

please...

no more."

but it was exactly as before
and so I stayed, silent
but I couldn't ignore
what approached my open door

On the Floor

like a dream in the morning
I want more

your peppermint poetry
smeared on phantom lips
November evenings
draped across your fingers
like silk and lace

hold on to me
and I'll hold you
I won't let you vanish
as long as you're home
in my arms

I want you
like a dream in the morning

A Dream in the Morning

my pretty poltergeist
we play
the most ghastly music together
the walls crack
and the floors creak
and the house shakes
to our dancing shoes
the neighbors don't catch a wink

my pretty poltergeist
we dance
in our evanescent embrace
memories of young love
twirl like toys in a typhoon
needles on records scratching songs of Samhain
the echoes of maniacal giggles and laughter
surround us in our haunted home

and we play
and we dance
forever

My Pretty Poltergeist

come to bed with me
flow into my open mouth
tumble down my throat
make my heart
your home

give me flowers to adorn my hours
delicate heads, nodding
to the sighing zephyr
wind chime bells, bending
lullabies of growth
in your hiding amaryllis
always take time
to open a window
bask in the sun
let in the rain

Hiding Amaryllis

oh honey
you fill my mouth
with bees crawling
over tongue and teeth
in buzzing ballets

collecting the pollen
from our rosebud hearts
and marigold souls
together we trade nectars
as they drip down our necks

Bees

latch on to me, my parasite
and never let go
absorb all that is mine
forever

you can have it all
everything I've become
and become just as I am
forever, my little parasite

Parasite

you were so kind
to reattach my head
your hand in mine
with thick black thread

we're stitched like a quilt
from the shoulder to the wrist
even as our lips wilt
we're still caught in our final kiss

what a great year
starting and ending with you
riding with the lunar sphere
towards an infinite view

Stitched

my haunted heart
painted red
with the roses
in your head

coil around my chest
slow and gentle
the lonely possessed
offer your body,
transcendental,
instill and thaw me

bind my hands
to hold nothing
but your starless strands
wafting on a voice
sweet and loving
not even death could destroy

coil my legs
lay me down
your warmth spreads
I'm not going anywhere
your flesh is my shroud
the only garments I wear

the Warmth of your Embrace

hold me
until you no longer fade away
and you're no longer a face
sweet and smoky

hold me
until you cannot pass through me
and you're more than a mist of beauty
a cold breeze

Hold Me

I'll never let you go
these doors will never close
the hallway candles glow
a beacon to bring you home

bed sheets cold and dry
flutter like butterflies
dressers decorated in corpses of flies
trying to remember your lullaby

you never went away
in my haunted heart, you lay
never will our love decay
even as this house begins to raze

As Our House Falls

snowdrops served on alabaster plates
cardinal tears in my throat
somehow elate me
with the arias you wrote

Cardinal Arias

while the wedding party
toasted the apocalypse
drinking their pink champagne
through gas mask canisters
the crow and the sparrow
dressed in their funeral attire
walked to the shore of the wreckage
waiting to be engaged to the tide

Forever

behind translucence
the shape of a hand appears
and elegant fingers
reveal the rest of you

caught in a gape
I can't bring myself
to utter any sound
only the emanating of heartbeats

that first movement
you stand in slow motion
delicately dripping
down vitreous skin

you step out
the legs of a dancer
we meet by silent invitation
in the center of the room

we are standing in a lake
while gravity takes over
no words
I'm drowning

before we trade oceans
on our tile shore
you ask me
"will you swim with me?"

I wake up
soaked
drenched
in dark-stained sheets

there's a faint taste
of lake shores and summer rain
and a trail of tiny pools
disappearing down the hall

Will You Swim With Me?

in the spotlight
performing your grand illusions
and disappearing acts
dancing to the rhythm
of my broken heart

it's a full house every night
I'm enthralled by your movements
as you leave ethereal tracks
I find myself dancing in them
while the theater falls apart

Dance of the Departed

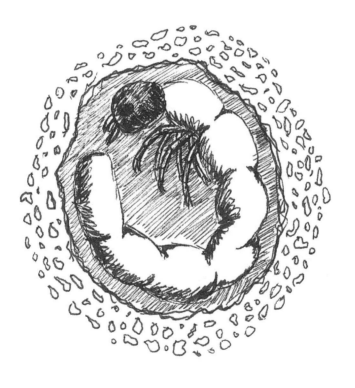

lit up like a torch
running
to catch the twilight
your firefly embers
dancing

I am a moth
drunk in the dusk
drawn to your stars
I've been wishing upon
all my life

twisting and turning
approaching
from the dark
to die in your eyes
to die in your light

The Moth and the Firefly

not gone
but missed
fingers lock
so you can't slip

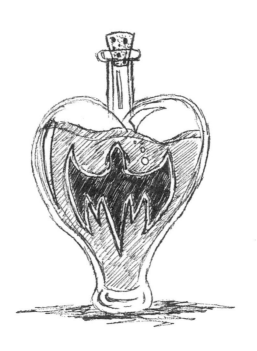

you held me close
just like before
and cooed
"I missed having you
in my life."

I looked deep
into your phantom eyes
and told you
"I miss
when you used to be alive."

crimson ribbons
around your ankles and wrists
burns permanent on soft skin
wrapped like a valentine gift

I remember you before your scars
were so much more distinct
headstones under your silk
overgrown with roses dripping pink

Silk and Headstones

winter hills of the desert sands
made of diamonds and pearls
adorning your lapel

you were never meant for human hands
like snow in December swirls
you will only melt

Fragile Snow

murder me in my dreams
never wake, stay asleep
open wide, absorb the screams
dug the grave six feet too deep

there's a difference between
who I am and what you see
stitch the skin over the scene
how can I escape from me?

I feel like I've said too much
our arms chain the gates
I get nervous when we touch
will we ever regenerate?

Regenerate

I am ash
painted on flesh
the patron saint of self-destruction
crumbling to dust
whenever we touch

I could take you home
but I know
you don't intend to stay long

do you prefer the alleys
dressed in graffiti and neon disease
singing your solivagant songs?

or the sewers
where your enemies are fewer
and you can lose yourself

I know these places
and their feuilleton faces
as well as you know yourself

Where You Call Home

you've lived here
for countless violent years
you're so scared
huddled under the stairs

angry ghosts turn wallpaper red
screaming in your haunted house head
you lit the wick to burn it down
effuming fog to smoke them out

but you got too high
now queen of the flies
in the ashes of the urn
forgetting who you were

Queen of the Flies

we throw skulls
at tombstone monuments
under twinkling neon stars
dancing to the songs of decades deceased

drinking from our nightshade nectars
stumbling over our bones and the caskets
of the thousands who have danced before us
we sit on the edge of an unmarked grave

and your arms coil around my waist
and I place your head on my shoulder
staring six feet down
I'm missing us already

Nightshade Nectar

this won't be like last time
would you like to hang your coat?
there's room in the closet
just push aside the meat
so they don't stain the fur

you must be thirsty
I'll pour you a glass
is there something wrong?
that's just a very fine chardonnay
you're not drinking

your skin shines
sparkling like a chandelier
covering you in crystal stars
your lips quiver, but I assure you
this won't be like last time

Chardonnay

can we meet again
before you depart once more?
river calling you
relentlessly
trickling poetic verse of longing

it's persistent
you know there is no resisting
but you're so tired
ready to rest on the river's bed
and I'm not ready to be alone

Ready To Be Alone

sleep well, my love
in the basement of my brain
one flickering bulb
the crickets' last refrain

I'll tuck you in
a blanket of threnody threads
over your cool blue skin
and lips still glossed in red

Crickets' Last Refrain

your name, a flourishing strand
on an elegant casket
like a plaque over a door
my dame of the damned
may your flesh be adorned with maggots
and your heart suffer no more

Flesh Adorned

rest now
tired soul
forget how fire
went so cold

sleep well
tired heart
the deep spell
and cries heard afar

wake soon
my love
lake moon
sky above

author photo by Jessica Kretzenger Photography

VINCENT HOLLOW is a poetic poltergeist rearranging his
hauntings and nightmares into tales of verse and prose, finding
inspiration in the songs of the stars and the music of mausoleums.

also by
Vincent Hollow

Swan Songs of Cygnus:
The Weight of Black Holes

Ghosts and other Vital Organs

CPSIA information can be obtained
at www.ICGtesting.com
Printed in the USA
BVHW081716110321
602276BV00003B/229